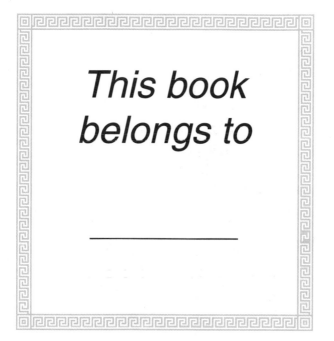

This book belongs to

_____

MY VERY FIRST
BOOK OF

BIBLE
LESSONS

MY VERY FIRST
BOOK OF

BIBLE
LESSONS

Mary Hollingsworth

Illustrated by
Rick Incrocci

THOMAS NELSON PUBLISHERS
Nashville

Dear Parents,

Thanks for choosing this book for your child. I hope you and your child enjoy it. I think you will because it has some great lessons in it. In fact, they are the most important lessons of life—lessons from God's Word. Nothing is more vital to your child's spiritual development than learning lessons from the Bible.

One of the most important features of this book is its simplicity. The book presents an entire Bible lesson in just one sentence. You'll find a new lesson every time you turn the page, each one perfect for the eyes, ears, and attention span of your young child.

Your child will like the colorful pictures in this book, too. Even if she can't read the words just yet, she can look at the pictures. So as you read the powerful words, your child can get the impact of the message from the pictures. If your child can read already, he can learn these lessons all by himself.

Why not settle down in a big chair with your child on your lap and learn some of the greatest lessons in the world together right now? I think you and your child will be blessed.

Mary Hollingsworth

The LORD God took the man and put him in the garden of Eden to tend and keep it.

Genesis 2:15

Learning to Care for My World

1. What are Jose and his dad doing in the picture? (Planting a tree.)
2. How are they taking care of the earth? (By putting back what they use.)
3. Ask your mom or dad to help you plant a new tree sometime soon.

Take care of the earth.

Do what is right and good in the sight of
the LORD.

Deuteronomy 6:18

Learning Right from Wrong

1. What does the sign in the picture say?
   (Stop.)
2. Is Jennifer doing what is right? (Yes.)
3. Why is it important to do what is
   right? (To be safe; to obey God.)

Always do what is right.

He is your praise, and He is your God.

Deuteronomy 10:21

Learning to Praise

1. Do these children look happy? (Yes.)
2. What are they doing that makes them happy? (Praising God.)
3. Will you be happy if you praise God, too? (Yes.)
4. Let's sing a song to praise God right now. Sing "God Is So Good."

**Praise God for the
wonderful things He does.**

> I will remember the works of the LORD.
> *Psalm 77:11*

Learning to Remember

1. Point to the baby Jesus in the picture.
2. Whose son is Jesus? (God's.)
3. Why did Jesus come to earth from heaven? (To save us.)
4. What can you do to remember that God sent Jesus to save us?

Always remember what
God has done for you.

Fear the LORD and depart from evil.

Proverbs 3:7

Learning to Stay Away from People Who Do Mean Things

1. Which boys in the picture do mean things? (The gang members.)
2. What is the other boy, Levon, doing? (Walking away.)
3. What should you do when someone wants you to do something bad? (Run!)

Stay away from people
who do mean things.

A friend loves at all times.

Proverbs 17:17

Learning to Be a Friend

1. Are these girls having fun together?
   (Yes.)
2. What do you enjoy doing with your
   friends?
3. Who is your best friend?

Be a good friend.

He who has a generous eye will be blessed,
for he gives of his bread to the poor.

Proverbs 22:9

Learning to Feed People Who Are Hungry

1. What are Chen and Connie doing for Bobby? (Giving him food.)
2. Is Bobby smiling? (Yes.)
3. How can you make a hungry person smile? (By giving him food.)

Give food to people who
are hungry.

25

The ants are a people not strong, yet they prepare their food in the summer.

Proverbs 30:25

Learning to Be a Good Worker

1. Are these ants working hard? (Yes.)
2. Why are these ants working so hard? (To get ready for winter.)
3. What kind of work do you do?

Be a good worker
like an ant.

Fear God and keep His commandments.
Ecclesiastes 12:13

Learning to Do What God Says

1. God said children should help people who are older. Is that what Manuel and Nikki are doing? (Yes.)
2. Are they keeping God's rules? (Yes.)
3. What can you do to keep God's rules?

Do everything God
says to do.

Those who wait on the LORD . . . shall mount up with wings like eagles.

Isaiah 40:31

Learning to Be Strong

1. Point to the eagle in the picture.
2. Is the eagle strong and brave? (Yes.)
3. Will God help you to be strong, too? (Yes.)
4. Would you like to fly like this eagle?

Be strong like an eagle.

Blessed are the peacemakers, for they shall be called sons of God.

Matthew 5:9

Learning to Make Peace

1. How is Michael helping his brother and sister make peace in this picture? (By helping them share and not fight.)
2. Does God like it when we fight? (No.)
3. How can you live in peace with your friends?

Help others live in peace.

Honor your father and your mother.

Matthew 15:4

Learning to Care for My Family

1. How is Helen taking care of her mother? (By brushing her hair.)
2. Do you honor your mother and dad when you help them? (Yes.)
3. What can you do to take care of your family?

Take care of your family.

You shall love your neighbor as yourself.
Matthew 19:19

Learning to Be a Good Neighbor

1. Are Juan and Maria being good neighbors? (Yes.)
2. Does it look like they are having fun? (Yes.)
3. What can you do as a good neighbor?
4. Can being a good neighbor be fun? (Yes.)

Be a good neighbor.

You shall love the LORD your God with all your heart, with all your soul, and with all your mind.

Matthew 22:37

Learning to Love God

1. Where are these children? (In church.)
2. Why do they go to church? (They love God.)
3. Do you love God with all your heart, too?
4. How can you show others that you love God?

Love God with all
your heart.

Love your enemies, do good to those who hate you.

Luke 6:27

Learning to Do Good

1. Does Tim have a black eye? (Yes.)
2. How do you think Tim got his black eye? (Someone hit him.)
3. What is Tim doing now? (Praying.) Whom is he praying for? (The one who hit him.)
4. Whom should you pray for?

Do good to people who
hurt you.

Well done, good servant; because you
were faithful in a very little, have
authority over ten cities.

Luke 19:17

Learning to Be Humble

1. Are some jobs more important than
   others? (Yes.)
2. God said to do little things well. Then
   He will give us important things to do.
   Do you like to do little things for God?
3. Erasing the blackboard is a little job.
   Does Sally look happy erasing the
   board? (Yes.)

Be happy to do little
things for God.

God so loved the world that He gave His only begotten Son, that whoever believes in Him should not perish but have everlasting life.

John 3:16

Learning to Believe

1. Point to Jesus in the picture.
2. Do you think Iva believes Jesus loves her? (Yes.) Why? (Thinking about Him makes her happy.)
3. Do you believe that Jesus loves you?

Believe that Jesus
loves you.

As I have loved you . . . you also love one another.

John 13:34

Learning to Love Others

1. Do the two friends in the picture love each other? (Yes.) How do you know? (They are hugging.)
2. Name everyone you love.
3. Give someone you love a hug right now.

Love other people.

I am ready to preach the gospel to you.
Romans 1:15

Learning to Tell the Good News

1. The gospel is the good news about Jesus. Does this good news make you happy?
2. Will the good news about Jesus make your friends happy? (Yes.)
3. Which of your friends would you like to tell about Jesus?

Tell the good news
to everyone.

If your enemy is . . . thirsty, give him a drink.

Romans 12:20

Learning to Help Thirsty People

1. What does a thirsty person need more than anything else? (Water.)
2. If Jesus saw a thirsty person, what would He do? (Give him a drink.)
3. If you see a thirsty person, what will you do?

Give water to thirsty
people.

Comfort those who are in any trouble, with the comfort with which we . . . are comforted by God.

2 Corinthians 1:4

Learning to Help People in Trouble

1. Jimmy is in trouble in this picture. What is wrong? (He is drowning.)
2. Is Laura helping him? (Yes.)
3. What would you do if you saw someone in trouble?
4. Have you ever helped someone who was in trouble?

Help people who are in
trouble.

God loves a cheerful giver.

2 Corinthians 9:7

Learning to Give

1. Joni's dad has given her an allowance. What is Joni doing with part of her allowance? (Giving it to God.)
2. Does God love for you to help people in need? (Yes.)
3. What can you give to help people in need?

Give cheerfully to
people in need.

Through love serve one another.
Galatians 5:13

Learning to Serve

1. Why is Johnny happy in this picture?
   (He's serving Mr. Chung.)
2. Does it make you happy to do nice
   things for other people?
3. What could you do to serve your mom
   or dad right now?

Be happy to serve other people.

Let each one of you speak truth with his neighbor.

Ephesians 4:25

Learning to Tell the Truth

1   What is Miko saying in this picture? ("I broke the window.")
2. Is it always easy to tell the truth? (No.)
3. Does it make God happy when you tell the truth? (Yes.)
4. Will you always try to tell the truth?

Always tell the truth.

Be kind to one another.

Ephesians 4:32

Learning to Be Kind

1. Is the woman in this picture sick?
   (Yes.)
2. Will these flowers make her feel better?
   (Yes.)
3. Are these children being kind to the
   woman by bringing her flowers? (Yes.)
4. Can you think of a time when you
   were kind to someone?

Be kind to people.

Children, obey your parents in the LORD,
for this is right.

Ephesians 6:1

Learning to Obey

1. What is Sancho doing in this picture?
   (Taking out the trash.)
2. Do you think Sancho's mom or dad
   asked him to take out the trash? (Yes.)
3. Does God smile when you do what
   your parents ask you to do? (Yes.)
4. Does it make your parents happy when
   you do what they ask you to do? (Yes.)

Obey your parents.

Rejoice always.
1 Thessalonians 5:16

Learning to Be Happy

1. Jesus loves all the children in the
   world. Does that make you happy?
2. If you always remember that Jesus loves
   you, can you always be happy? (Yes.)
3. Let's sing a happy song about Jesus'
   love. Sing "Jesus Loves the Little
   Children."

Be happy always.

Pray without ceasing.
1 Thessalonians 5:17

Learning to Pray

1. What are the children doing in the picture? (Praying.)
2. Is it all right to pray to God anytime you want to? (Yes.)
3. Does praying to God make you happy?
4. Let's pray to God right now.

Pray all the time.

Let them do good, that they be rich in good works, ready to give, willing to share.

1 Timothy 6:18

Learning to Share

1. Do you like for your friends to share with you?
2. Does it make God happy to see you sharing with others? (Yes.)
3. What do you have that you can share with your friends?

Share with others.

Be diligent to present yourself approved to God . . . rightly dividing the word of truth.
2 Timothy 2:15

Learning to Study

1. The Bible is God's word. Should you study the Bible every day? (Yes.)
2. Does God like to see you learning about His word? (Yes.)
3. Do you love God and the Bible?

Study the Bible
every day.

Let everyone who names the name of
Christ depart from iniquity.

2 Timothy 2:19

Learning to Say No

1. What is the big girl in the picture
   trying to get Benita to do? (Take
   drugs.)
2. What should Benita do? (Run!)
3. What should you do if someone tries
   to get you to do something harmful?
   (Run!)

Stay away from things
that can harm you.

A servant of the LORD must . . . be gentle to all.

2 Timothy 2:24

Learning to Be Gentle

1. Is Marco being gentle with the little yellow duckling? (Yes.)
2. What sound does the duckling make when it is happy? (Quack, quack.)
3. Does the duckling like being held gently? (Yes.)
4. Are you gentle with others?

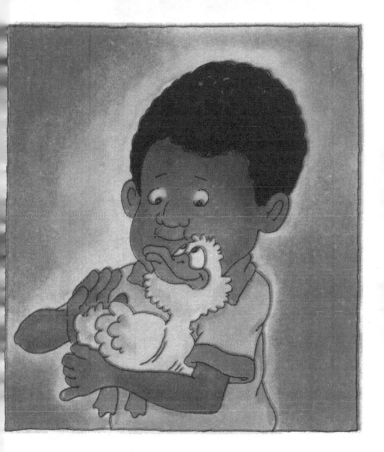

Be gentle.

Remember the prisoners as if chained with them.

Hebrews 13:3

Learning to Be Thoughtful

1. Are people in prison lonely and sad? (Yes.)
2. What is Sian doing in the picture? (Writing a letter to a prisoner.)
3. Will the prisoner be happy to get Sian's letter? (Yes.)
4. Would you like to write a letter to a prisoner, too?

Remember people who
are in prison.

Do not forget to do good and to share.
Hebrews 13:16

Learning to Do Good

1. Bret is giving Zina one of his new puppies. Is that a good thing to do? (Yes.)
2 Does it make you happy to do good things for other people?
3. What good thing can you do right now?

Do good things
for people.

Visit orphans . . . in their trouble.

James 1:27

Learning to Love Children Who Have No Parents

1. Some children do not have any parents. Could a child who has no parents use a good friend like you? (Yes.)
2. How could you show someone who has no parents that you want to be friends?
3. Could you invite a child who has no parents to visit in your home and share your family for a while?

Be kind to children who
have no parents.

Is anyone cheerful? Let him sing psalms.

James 5:13

Learning to Sing

1. Do you like to sing?
2. How does singing a happy song make you feel?
3. Let's sing a happy song right now. Sing "I'm Happy Today."

Sing with a happy heart.

Always be ready to give a defense to everyone who asks you a reason for the hope that is in you.

1 Peter 3:15

Learning to Witness

1. Point to God's Word in the picture.
2. What do you think Letitia is talking about to Grace? (God.)
3. If your best friend asked you why you love God, what would you say?

Be ready to tell people
why you love God.

You younger people, submit yourselves to your elders.

1 Peter 5:5

Learning to Respect People Who Are Older

1. Why is the woman in the picture smiling? (She is being helped.)
2. Is Traci being respectful to her? (Yes.)
3. How can you show respect to people who are older than you, such as your parents and grandparents?

Respect people who are
older; they are wise.

God resists the proud, but gives grace to
the humble.

1 Peter 5:5

Learning to Be Humble

1. Do you like for your best friend to brag?
2. How does it make you feel when your friend brags about something?
3. Does God smile when we brag about ourselves? (No.)
4. Jesus was God's Son, but He didn't brag about it. Will you try to be humble like Jesus?

Be humble about what
you do; don't brag.

Blessed is he who reads and those who hear the words of this prophecy, and keep those things which are written in it.

Revelation 1:3

Learning How to Be Happy

1. Is Chou happy in this picture? (Yes.)
2. Why do you think he is happy? (He is reading the Bible.)
3. What can you do to be happy like Chou?
4. Let's read the Bible right now.

Read God's Word, and
you will be happy.

91

Other books in this series

My Very First Book of Bible Words

My Very First Book of Prayers

My Very First Book of Bible Heroes